SONGS OF THE
1920s

 100 Songs with Online Audio Backing Tracks

To access audio visit:
www.halleonard.com/mylibrary

Enter Code
8162-6034-6750-8162

ISBN 978-1-4950-0024-9

HAL•LEONARD®
CORPORATION

7777 W. BLUEMOUND RD. P.O. BOX 13819 MILWAUKEE, WI 53213

Visit Hal Leonard Online at
www.halleonard.com

AIN'T MISBEHAVIN'

Words by ANDY RAZAF
Music by THOMAS "FATS" WALLER
and HARRY BROOKS

AMONG MY SOUVENIRS

Words by EDGAR LESLIE
Music by HORATIO NICHOLAS

Slowly, with expression

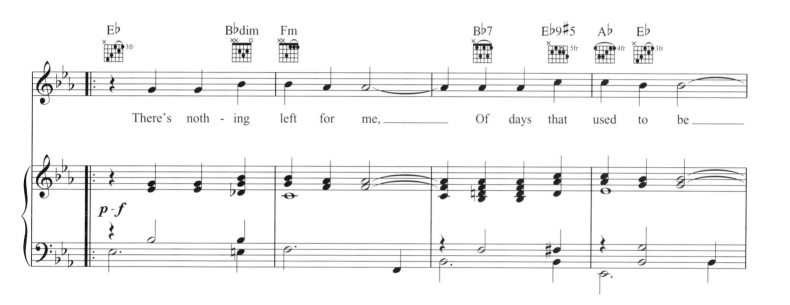

There's noth-ing left for me, ____ Of days that used to be ____

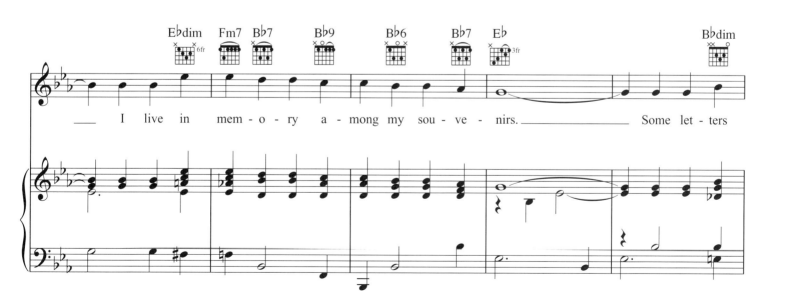

____ I live in mem-o-ry a-mong my sou-ve-nirs. ____ Some let-ters

tied with blue, _____ A pho-to-graph or two, _____ I see a rose from you a-

mong my sou-ve-nirs. _____ A few more to-kens rest _____ with-in my

treas-ure chest, _____ And though they do their best _____ To give me

con - so - la - tion, I count them all a - part, _____ And as the

tear - drops start, _____ I find a bro - ken heart a - mong my sou - ve -

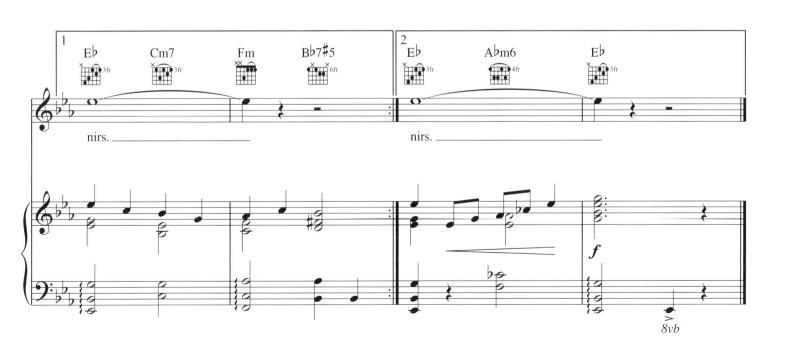

nirs. _____ nirs. _____

ALL ALONE

Words and Music by
IRVING BERLIN

ALWAYS

Words and Music by
IRVING BERLIN

Moderate Waltz

Ev - 'ry - thing went wrong, and the whole day long I'd
Dreams will all come true, grow - ing old with you, and

feel so blue.
time will fly,

APRIL SHOWERS

Words by B.G. DeSYLVA
Music by LOUIS SILVERS

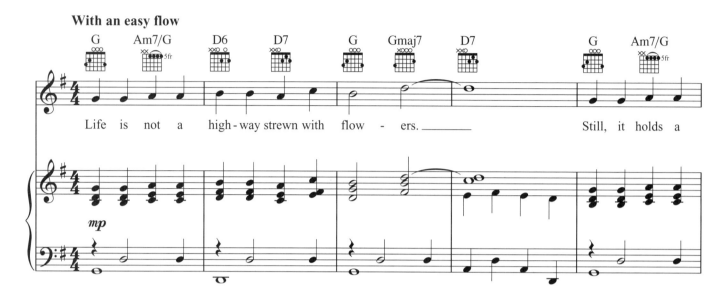

BASIN STREET BLUES

Words and Music by
SPENCER WILLIAMS

24

BABY FACE

Words and Music by BENNY DAVIS
and HARRY AKST

BACK IN YOUR OWN BACKYARD

Words and Music by AL JOLSON,
BILLY ROSE and DAVE DREYER

THE BEST THINGS IN LIFE ARE FREE

Music and Lyrics by B.G. DeSYLVA,
LEW BROWN and RAY HENDERSON

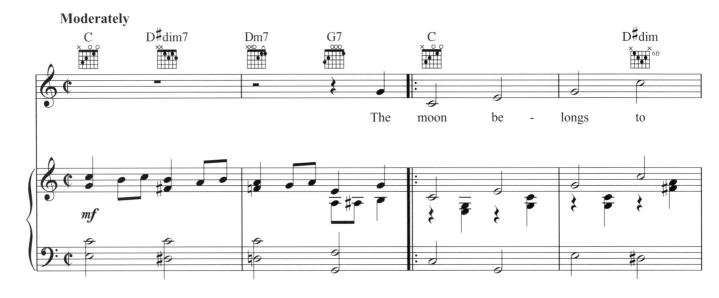

The moon be - longs to

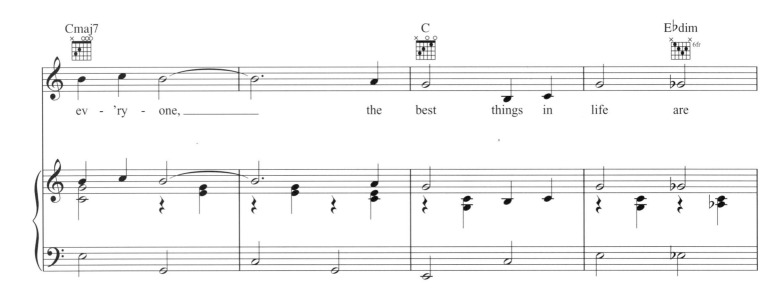

ev - 'ry - one, _____ the best things in life are

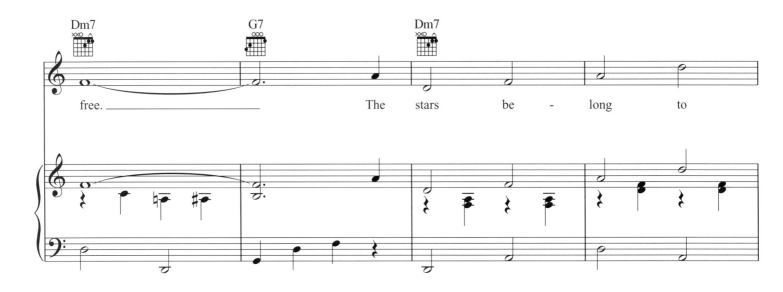

free. _____ The stars be - long to

BILL
from SHOW BOAT

Music by JEROME KERN
Words by P.G. WODEHOUSE
and OSCAR HAMMERSTEIN II

I used to dream that I would dis-cov-er ___ the per-fect
He can't play golf, or ten-nis, or po-lo, ___ or sing a

lov-er some day. I knew I'd re-cog-nize him if
so-lo, or row. He is-n't half as hand-some as

ev-er he came 'round my way. I
doz-ens of men 'round that I know. He

THE BIRTH OF THE BLUES

Words by B.G. DeSYLVA and LEW BROWN
Music by RAY HENDERSON

44

BUTTON UP YOUR OVERCOAT

Words and Music by B.G. DeSYLVA,
LEW BROWN and RAY HENDERSON

Lyrics:

But-ton up your o-ver-coat
But-ton up your o-ver-coat

when the wind is free.
when the wind is free.

Take good
Take good

care of your-self you be-long to me!
care of your-self you be-long to me!

BLUE SKIES

Words and Music by
IRVING BERLIN

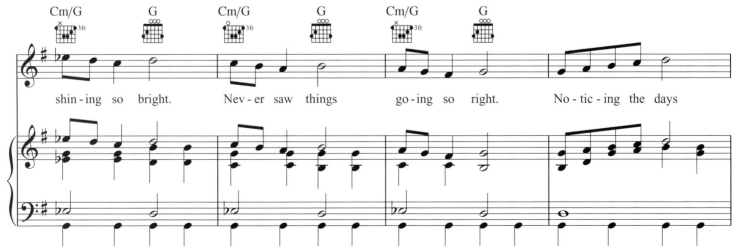

BYE BYE BLACKBIRD

Lyric by MORT DIXON
Music by RAY HENDERSON

CALIFORNIA, HERE I COME

Words and Music by AL JOLSON,
B.G. DeSYLVA and JOSEPH MEYER

CAN'T HELP LOVIN' DAT MAN

from SHOW BOAT

Lyrics by OSCAR HAMMERSTEIN II
Music by JEROME KERN

Slowly

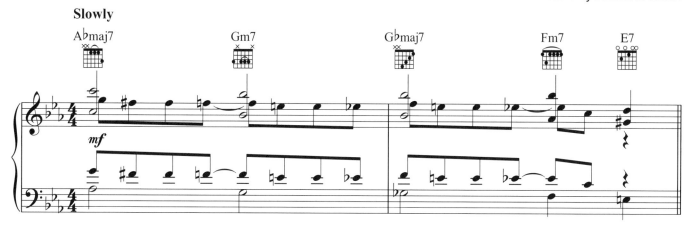

Fish got to swim___ and birds got to fly,___ I got to love___ one
Tell me he's la - zy, tell me he's slow,___ tell me I'm cra - zy,

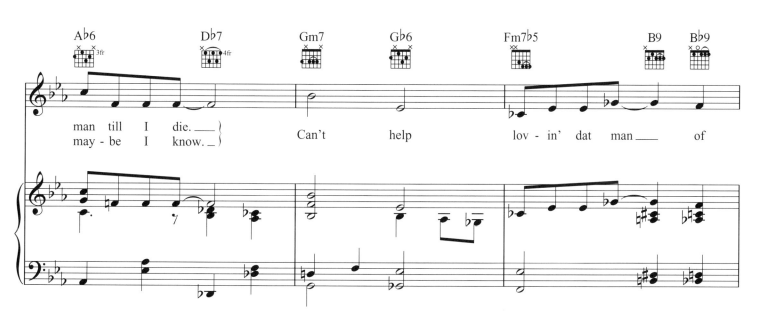

man till I die.___ Can't help lov - in' dat man___ of
may - be I know.___

62

CHARLESTON

Words and Music by CECIL MACK
and JIMMY JOHNSON

FASCINATING RHYTHM

Music and Lyrics by GEORGE GERSHWIN
and IRA GERSHWIN

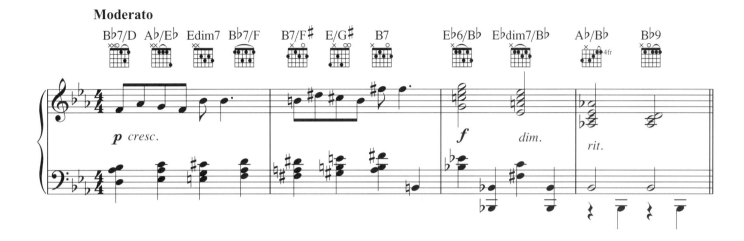

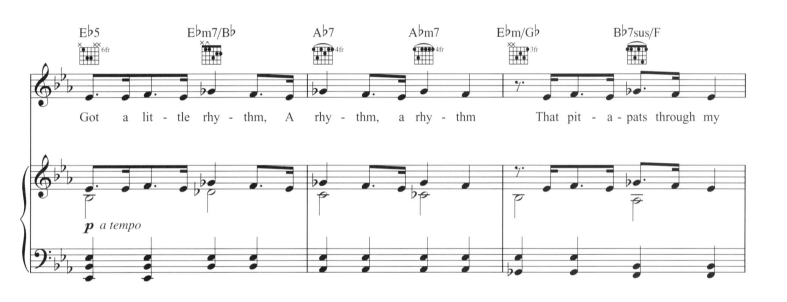

Got a lit-tle rhy-thm, A rhy-thm, a rhy-thm That pit-a-pats through my

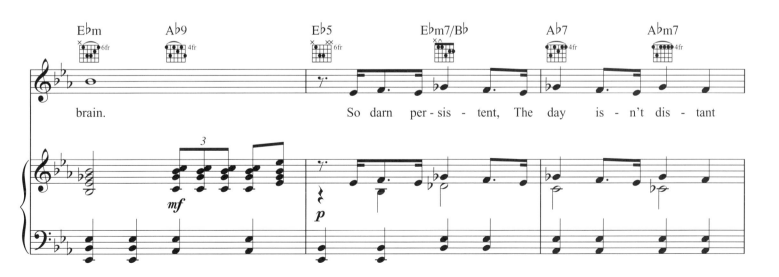

brain. So darn per-sis-tent, The day is-n't dis-tant

CHARMAINE

Words and Music by LEW POLLACK
and ERNO RAPEE

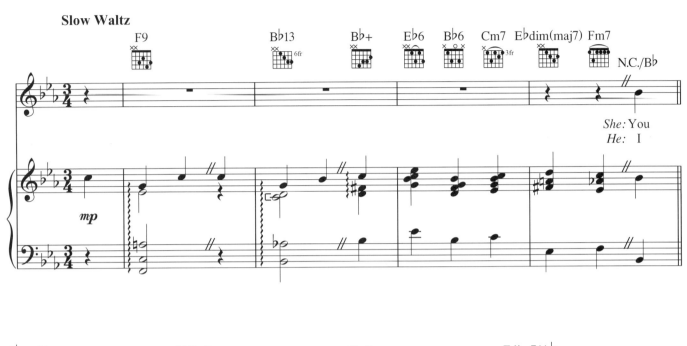

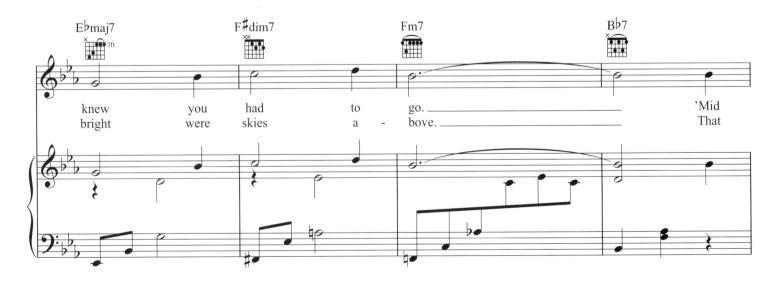

CRAZY RHYTHM
from THE COTTON CLUB

Words by IRVING CAESAR
Music by JOSEPH MEYER and ROGER WOLFE KAHN

'DEED I DO

Words and Music by WALTER HIRSCH
and FRED ROSE

EVERYBODY LOVES MY BABY
(But My Baby Don't Love Nobody but Me)

Words and Music by JACK PALMER
and SPENCER WILLIAMS

FIVE FOOT TWO, EYES OF BLUE
(Has Anybody Seen My Girl?)

Words by JOE YOUNG and SAM LEWIS
Music by RAY HENDERSON

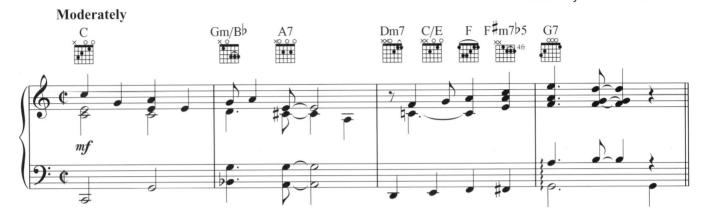

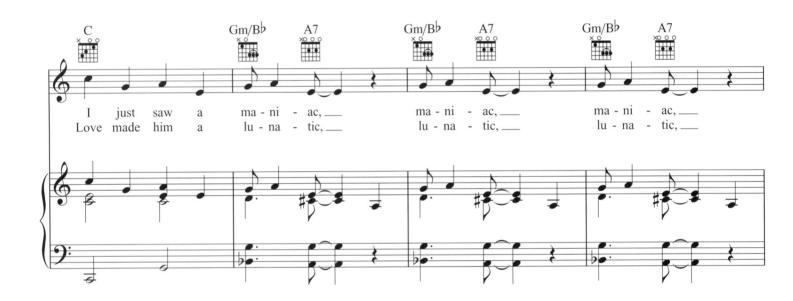

I just saw a ma-ni-ac, ___ ma-ni-ac, ___ ma-ni-ac, ___
Love made him a lu-na-tic, ___ lu-na-tic, ___ lu-na-tic, ___

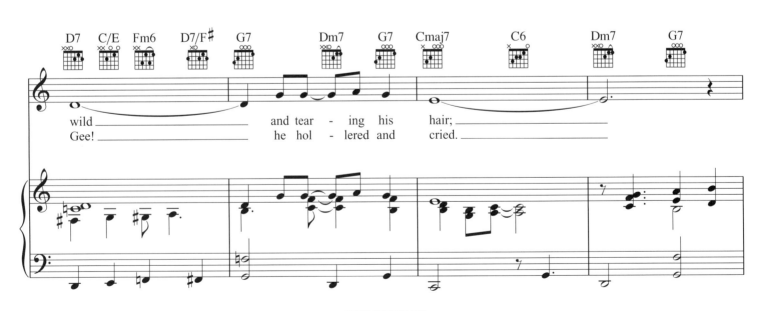

wild ___ and tear - ing his hair; ___
Gee! ___ he hol - lered and cried. ___

HONEYSUCKLE ROSE

Words by ANDY RAZAF
Music by THOMAS "FATS" WALLER

I CRIED FOR YOU

Words and Music by ARTHUR FREED,
GUS ARNHEIM and ABE LYMAN

HOW LONG HAS THIS BEEN GOING ON?

Music and Lyrics by GEORGE GERSHWIN
and IRA GERSHWIN

Bill: As a tot, when I trot-ted in lit-tle vel-vet pant - ies, _____
Mary: 'Neath the stars, at ba-zaars, of-ten I've had to ca-ress men. _____

I was kissed by my sis-ters, my cous-ins and my aunt-ies. _____
Five or ten dol-lars, then, I'd col-lect from all those yes - men. _____

Sad to tell, it was Hell, an in-fer-no worse than Dan-te's. _____
Don't be sad; I must add that they meant no more than chess - men. _____

I CAN'T BELIEVE THAT YOU'RE IN LOVE WITH ME

Words and Music by JIMMY McHUGH
and CLARENCE GASKILL

I CAN'T GIVE YOU ANYTHING BUT LOVE

Words and Music by JIMMY McHUGH
and DOROTHY FIELDS

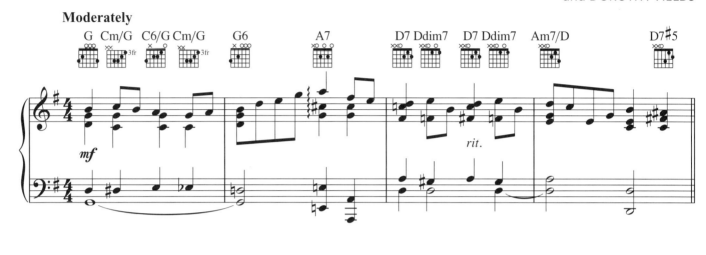

Gee, but it's tough to be broke, kid. ___ It's not a joke, kid, it's a

Rome was-n't built in a day, kid. ___ You have to pay, kid, ___ for what you

curse.

get.

My luck is chang-ing, it's got-ten ___ from sim-ply

But I am will-ing to wait, dear; ___ your lit-tle

I WANNA BE LOVED BY YOU

from GOOD BOY

Lyric by BERT KALMAR
Music by HERBERT STOTHART and HARRY RUBY

I WANT TO BE HAPPY

Words by IRVING CAESAR
Music by VINCENT YOUMANS

I'm a ver-y or-di-nar-y man, try-ing to work out life's
No one ev-er talked like that to me. I have nev-er known such

hap-py plan, do-ing un-to oth-ers as I'd like to have them do-ing un-to
sym-pa-thy. On-ly in my dreams, it real-ly seems to me it's too good to be

me. When I find a ver-y
true. There are smil-ing fac-es

I'LL GET BY
(As Long as I Have You)

Lyric by ROY TURK
Music by FRED E. AHLERT

I'LL SEE YOU IN MY DREAMS

Words by GUS KAHN
Music by ISHAM JONES

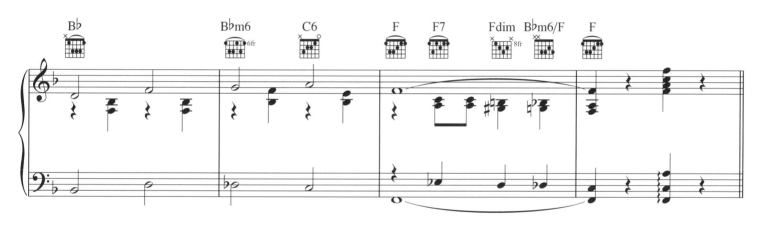

Though the days are long,   twi-light sings a song
In the drear-y grey   of an-oth-er day,

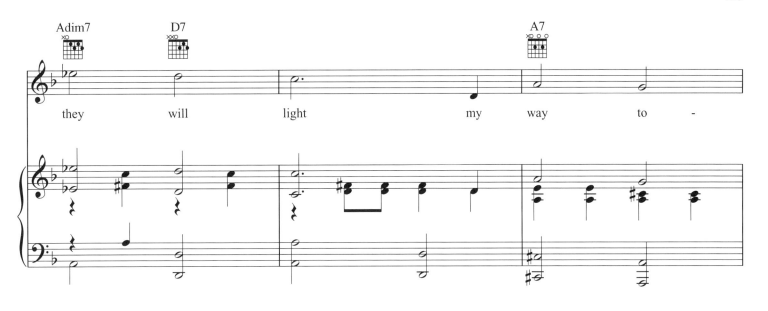

they will light my way to -

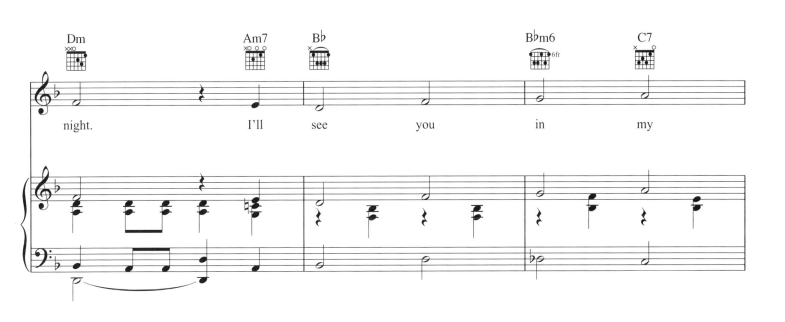

night. I'll see you in my

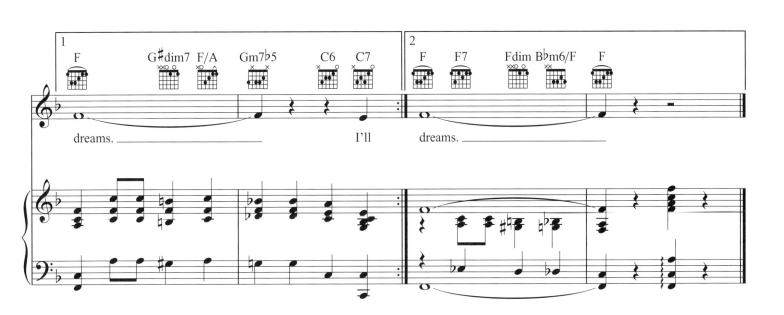

dreams. I'll dreams.

I'M SITTING ON TOP OF THE WORLD

Words by SAM M. LEWIS and JOE YOUNG
Music by RAY HENDERSON

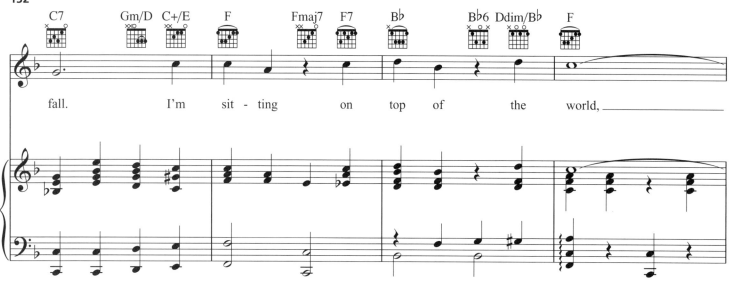

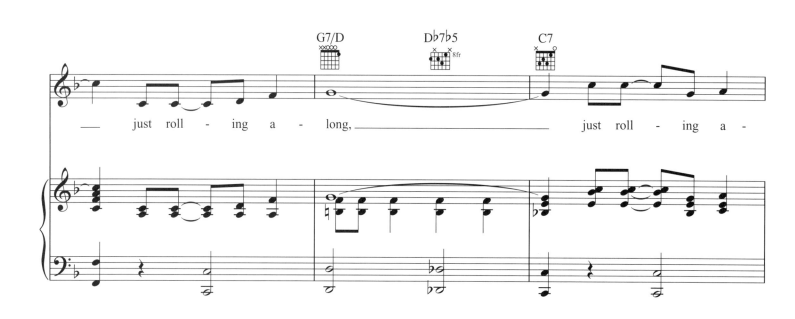

IF I COULD BE WITH YOU
(One Hour Tonight)

Words and Music by HENRY CREAMER
and JIMMY JOHNSON

IF I HAD YOU

Words and Music by TED SHAPIRO,
JIMMY CAMPBELL and REG CONNELLY

IF YOU KNEW SUSIE
(Like I Know Susie)

Words and Music by B.G. DeSYLVA
and JOSEPH MEYER

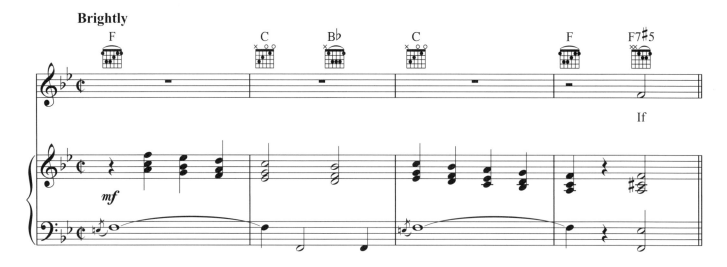

you knew Su - sie like I know Su - sie,

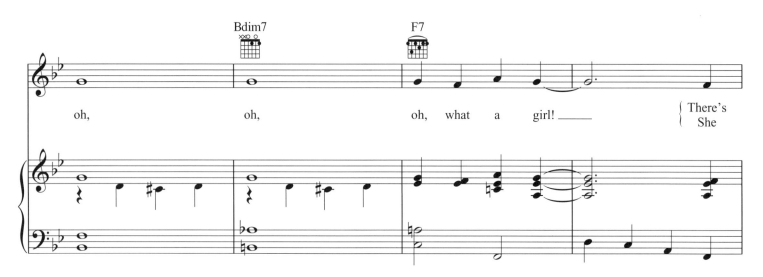

oh, oh, oh, what a girl! ____ { There's She

IT ALL DEPENDS ON YOU

Words and Music by B.G. DeSYLVA,
LEW BROWN and RAY HENDERSON

IN A LITTLE SPANISH TOWN
('Twas on a Night Like This)

Words by SAM M. LEWIS and JOE YOUNG
Music by MABEL WAYNE

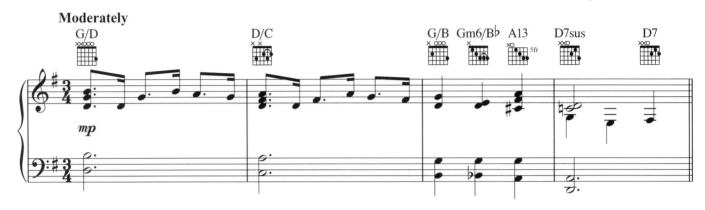

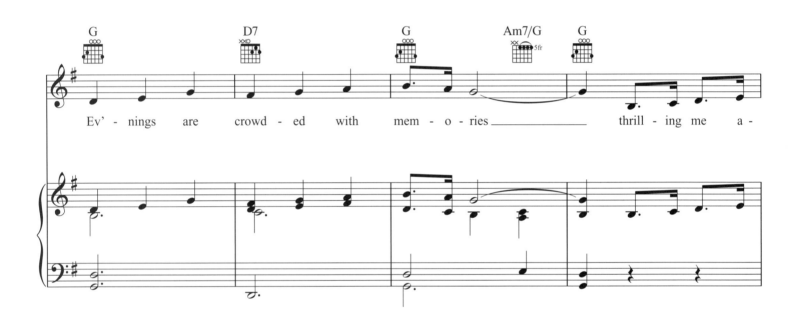

Ev'-nings are crowd-ed with mem-o-ries _____ thrill-ing me a-

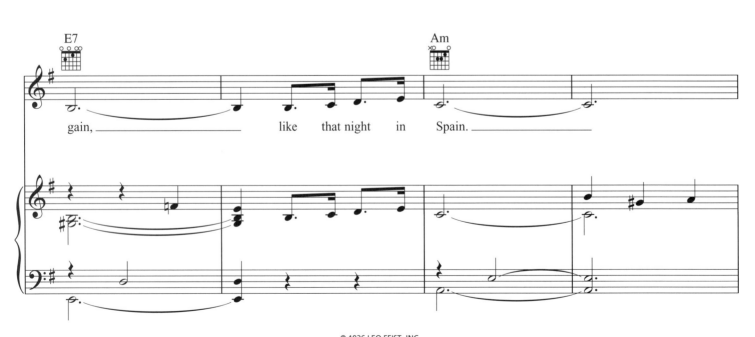

gain, _____ like that night in Spain. _____

IT HAD TO BE YOU

Words by GUS KAHN
Music by ISHAM JONES

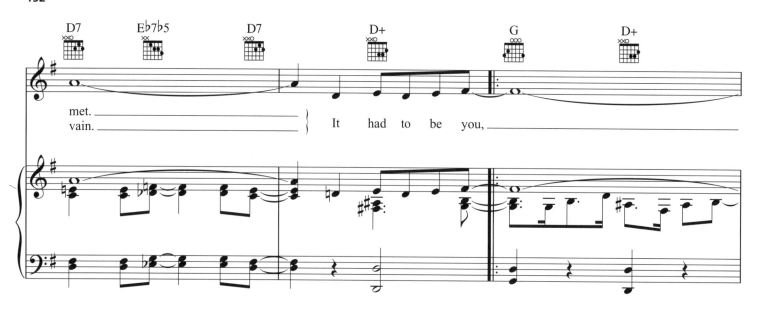

met. _____
vain. _____ } It had to be you, _____

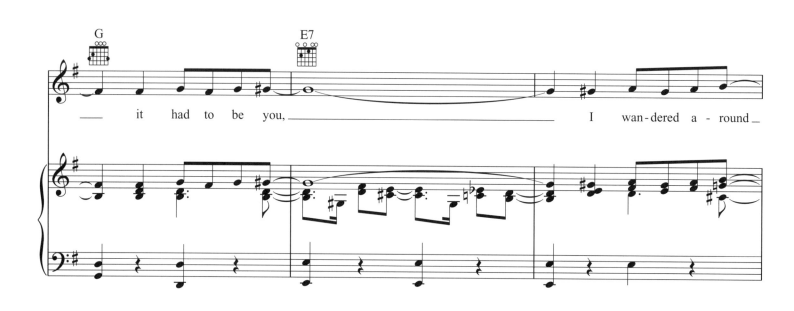

___ it had to be you, _____ I wan-dered a - round __

___ and fi - nal - ly found __ the some-bod - y who _____

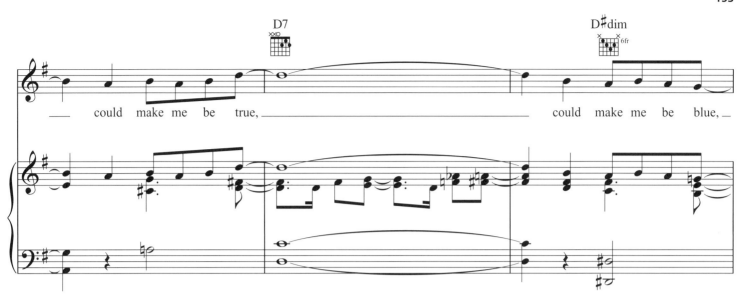

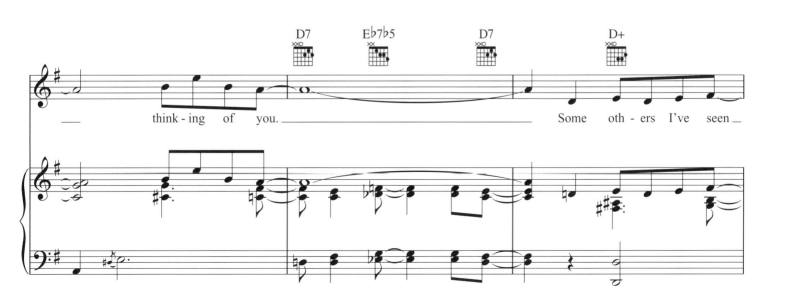

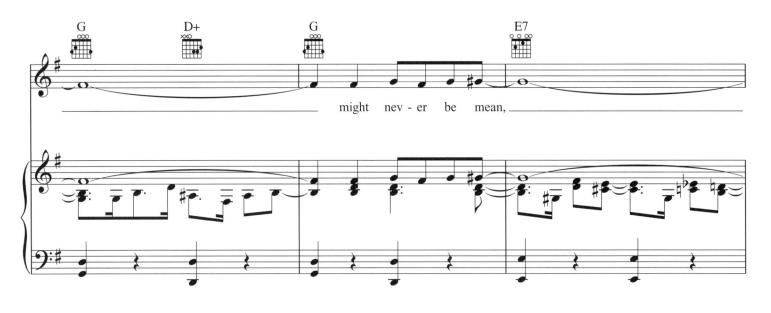

might nev-er be mean,

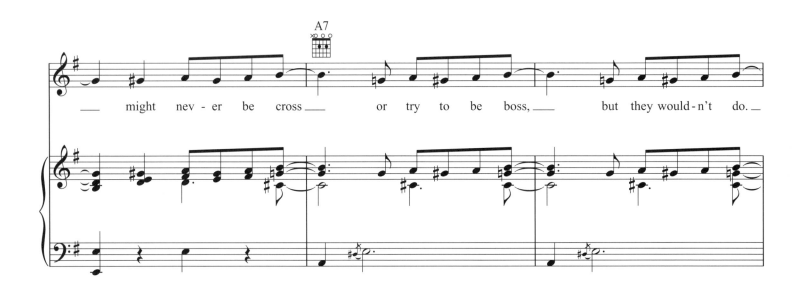

might nev-er be cross ___ or try to be boss, ___ but they would-n't do. ___

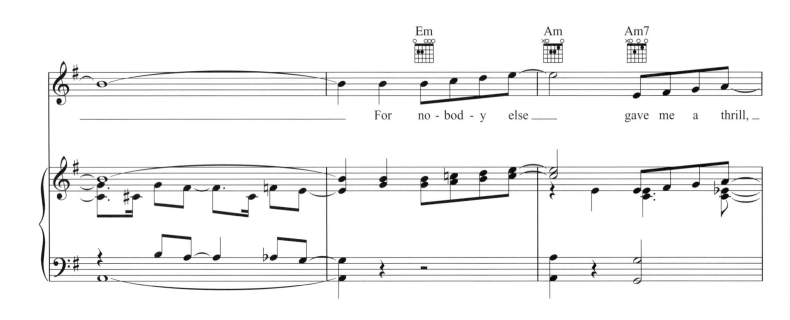

For no-bod-y else ___ gave me a thrill, ___

JUST YOU, JUST ME

Music by JESSE GREER
Lyrics by RAYMOND KLAGES

LET A SMILE BE YOUR UMBRELLA

Words by IRVING KAHAL and FRANCIS WHEELER
Music by SAMMY FAIN

LIZA
(All the Clouds'll Roll Away)

Music by GEORGE GERSHWIN
Lyrics by IRA GERSHWIN and GUS KAHN

166

167

LOOK FOR THE SILVER LINING

Words by BUDDY DeSYLVA
Music by JEROME KERN

MAKE BELIEVE

from SHOW BOAT

Lyrics by OSCAR HAMMERSTEIN II
Music by JEROME KERN

LOUISE

Words by LEO ROBIN
Music by RICHARD A. WHITING

178

LOVE ME OR LEAVE ME

Words by GUS KAHN
Music by WALTER DONALDSON

LOVER, COME BACK TO ME

from THE NEW MOON

Lyrics by OSCAR HAMMERSTEIN II
Music by SIGMUND ROMBERG

MACK THE KNIFE
from THE THREEPENNY OPERA

English Words by MARC BLITZSTEIN
Original German Words by BERT BRECHT
Music by KURT WEILL

MAKIN' WHOOPEE!

Lyrics by GUS KAHN
Music by WALTER DONALDSON

THE MAN I LOVE

Music and Lyrics by GEORGE GERSHWIN
and IRA GERSHWIN

MANHATTAN

Words by LORENZ HART
Music by RICHARD RODGERS

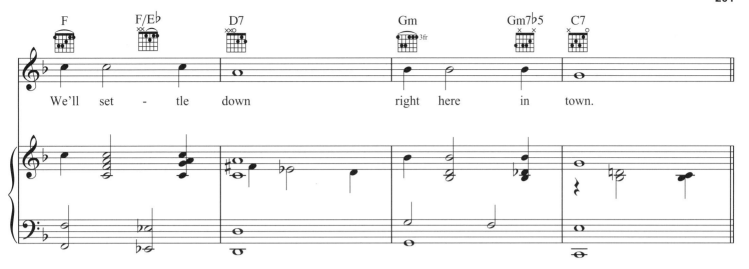

We'll set - tle down right here in town.

We'll have Man - hat - tan, the Bronx and Stat - en Is - land too; _____ It's love - ly
We'll go to Green - wich where mod - ern men itch to be free; _____ And Bowl - ing
We'll go to Yon - kers where true love con - quers in the wilds; _____ And starve to -
We'll have Man - hat - tan, the Bronx and Stat - en Is - land too; _____ We'll try to

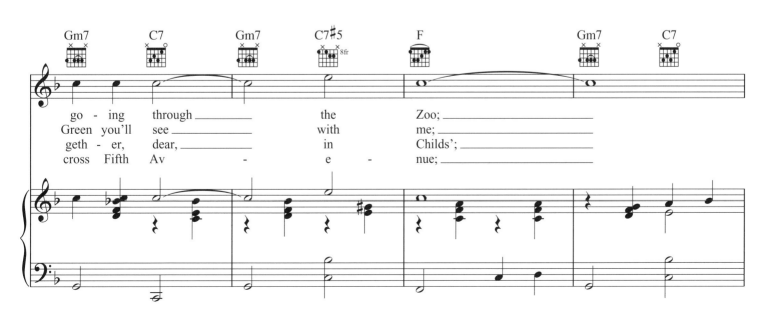

go - ing through _____ the Zoo; _____
Green you'll see _____ with me; _____
geth - er, dear, _____ in Childs'; _____
cross Fifth Av - e - nue; _____

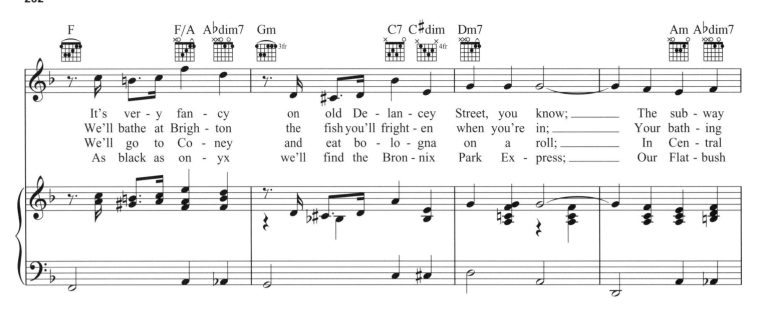

It's ver - y fan - cy on old De - lan - cey Street, you know; _____ The sub - way
We'll bathe at Brigh - ton the fish you'll fright - en when you're in; _____ Your bath - ing
We'll go to Co - ney and eat bo - lo - gna on a roll; _____ In Cen - tral
As black as on - yx we'll find the Bron - ix Park Ex - press; _____ Our Flat - bush

charms us so, _____ when balm - y breez - es blow to and fro; And tell me what street
suit so thin _____ will make the shell-fish grin fin to fin; I'd like to take a
Park, we'll stroll _____ where our first kiss we stole, soul to soul; And for some high fare
flat, I guess, _____ will be a great suc - cess, more or less. A short va - ca - tion

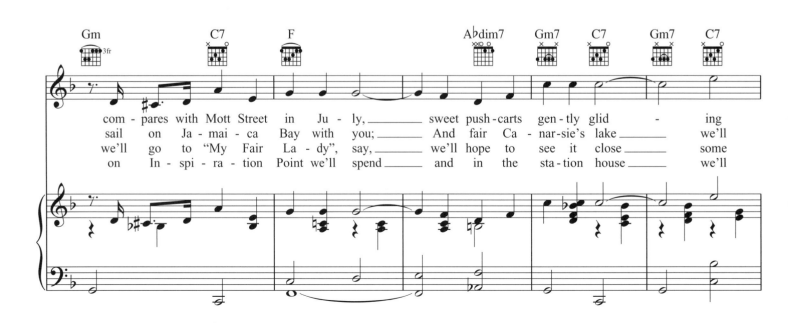

com - pares with Mott Street in Ju - ly, _____ sweet push-carts gen - tly glid - ing
sail on Ja - mai - ca Bay with you; _____ And fair Ca - nar-sie's lake _____ we'll
we'll go to "My Fair La - dy", say, _____ we'll hope to see it close _____ some
on In - spi - ra - tion Point we'll spend _____ and in the sta - tion house _____ we'll

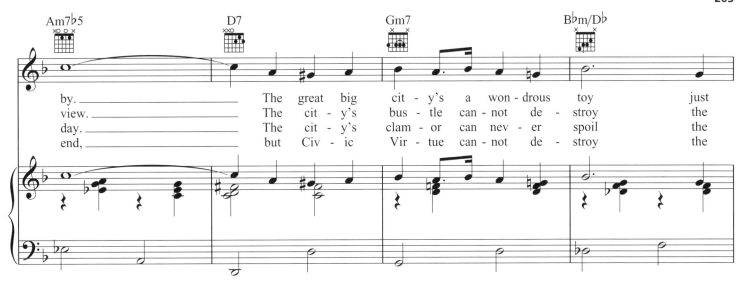

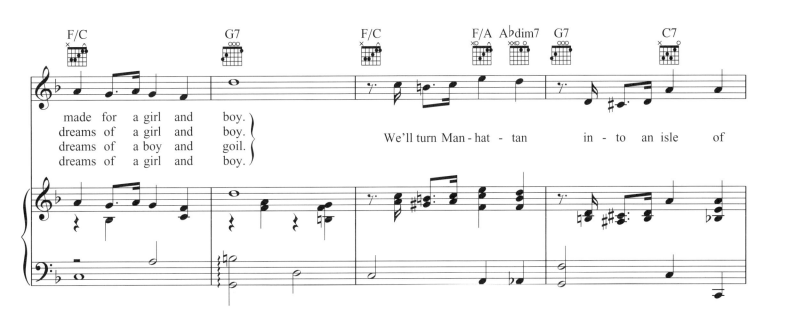

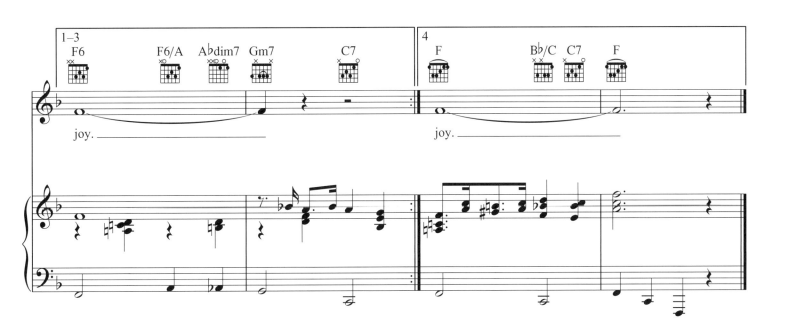

ME AND MY SHADOW

Words by BILLY ROSE
Music by AL JOLSON and DAVE DREYER

MORE THAN YOU KNOW

Words by WILLIAM ROSE and EDWARD ELISCU
Music by VINCENT YOUMANS

Slowly, with expression

More than you know, more than you know, (man)(girl) o' my heart, I love you so. Late-ly I find you're on my mind, more than you know. _____ Wheth-er you're

MEAN TO ME

Lyric by ROY TURK
Music by FRED E. AHLERT

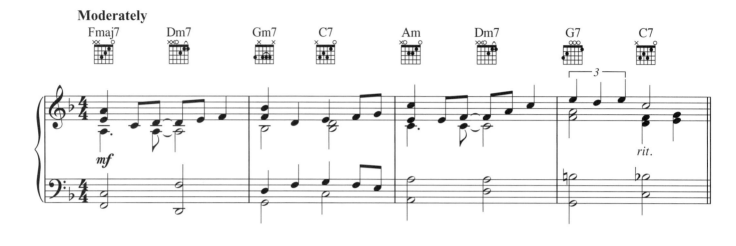

Sweet-heart I love __ you, think the world of __ you, but I'm a-fraid __ you don't
I treat you sweet-ly, I'm yours com-plete-ly, think of you, dream __ of you

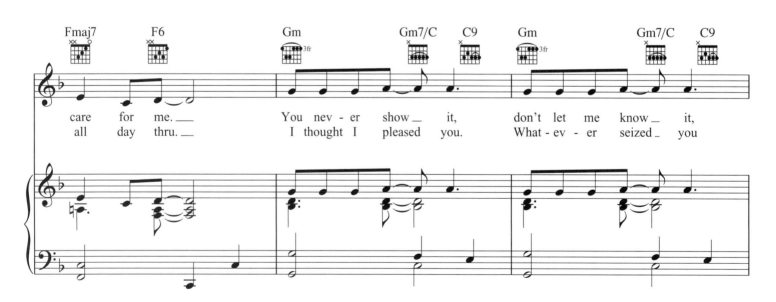

care for me. __ You nev-er show __ it, don't let me know __ it,
all day thru. __ I thought I pleased you. What-ev-er seized __ you

MISSISSIPPI MUD

Words and Music by JAMES CAVANAUGH
and HARRY BARRIS

When the sun goes down, the tide goes out, the peo-ple gath-er 'round and they all be-gin to shout: "Hey! Hey!

MOONLIGHT AND ROSES
(Bring Mem'ries of You)

Words and Music by BEN BLACK,
EDWIN LEMARE and NEIL MORET

Moon - light and ros - es _____ bring won - der - ful mem-'ries of you. _____ My heart re - pos - es _____ in beau - ti - ful thoughts so true. _____

June light dis - clos - es _____ love's old - en dreams spar - kling a - new. _____ Moon - light and ros - es _____ bring mem - 'ries _____ of you. _____ you. _____

MOUNTAIN GREENERY

from the Broadway Musical THE GARRICK GAIETIES

Words by LORENZ HART
Music by RICHARD RODGERS

MUSKRAT RAMBLE

Written by EDWARD ORY
and RAY GILBERT

Sev-en-o-nine,__ huff-in' and puff-in' and ar-riv-in' on time.__
tain-in' the gang,__ cling-ing and clang-ing with a bing and a bang!__

Who do you think's a-bout to 'rive?__ The band__ they call "The Dix-ie-land
Chang-ing the town from dead to 'live! The band__ they call "The Dix-ie-land

Five." They're gon-na play that musk-rat
Five." You're gon-na hear them play that

ram-ble tune, the way you nev-er ev-er heard it played.__
Dix-ie-land, you bet-ter get your res-er-va-tion planned,__

MY BLUE HEAVEN

Lyric by GEORGE WHITING
Music by WALTER DONALDSON

MY HEART STOOD STILL
from A CONNECTICUT YANKEE

Words by LORENZ HART
Music by RICHARD RODGERS

He: I laughed at sweet - hearts
She: Through all my school - days

I met at schools;
I hat - ed boys;
All in - dis - creet hearts
Those A - pril Fool days

Seemed ro - man - tic fools.
Brought me love - less joys.
A house in
I read my

MY MAN
(Mon homme)

Words by ALBERT WILLEMETZ and JACQUES CHARLES
English Words by CHANNING POLLOCK
Music by MAURICE YVAIN

It's cost me a lot, but there's one thing that I've got it's my man, __
Some-times I say if I just could get a-way with my man, __
Sur cet-te terr', ma seul' joie, mon seul bon-heur c'est mon hom-me

cold and wet, tired, you bet, but all that I soon for-get with my man. __
he'd go straight sure as fate, for it nev-er is too late for my man. __
J'ai don-né tout c'que j'ai, mon a-mour et tout mon cœur, a mon hom-me,

He's not much for looks, and no he-ro out of books is my man. __
I just like to dream of a cot-tage by a stream with my man, __
Et mê-me la nuit quand je rê-ve c'est de lui, de mon hom-me.

OL' MAN RIVER

from SHOW BOAT

Lyrics by OSCAR HAMMERSTEIN II
Music by JEROME KERN

OH, LADY BE GOOD!

from LADY, BE GOOD!

Music and Lyrics by GEORGE GERSHWIN
and IRA GERSHWIN

Allegretto grazioso

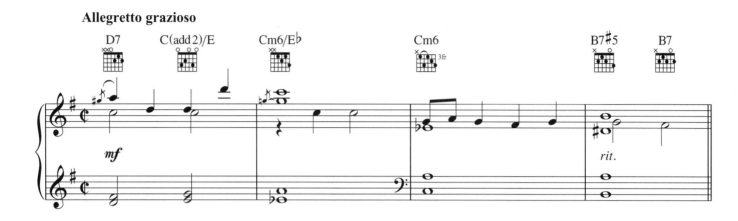

Calmly

Lis- ten to my tale of woe, It's ter-ri-bly sad, but
Au- burn and bru- nette and blonde: I love 'em all, tall or

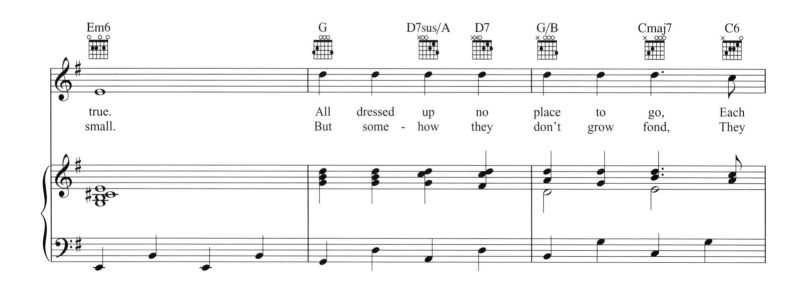

true. All dressed up no place to go, Each
small. But some- how they don't grow fond, They

PUTTIN' ON THE RITZ

Words and Music by
IRVING BERLIN

RAMONA

Words by L. WOLFE GILBERT
Music by MABEL WAYNE

RHAPSODY IN BLUE

By GEORGE GERSHWIN

Grandioso ma non troppo

ROCKIN' CHAIR

Words and Music by
HOAGY CARMICHAEL

'S WONDERFUL

Music and Lyrics by GEORGE GERSHWIN
and IRA GERSHWIN

ST. LOUIS BLUES

Words and Music by
W.C. HANDY

Extra Choruses (optional)

Lawd, a blonde-headed woman makes a good man leave the town,
I said a blonde-headed woman makes a good man leave the town,
But a red-head woman makes a boy slap his papa down.

O ashes to ashes and dust to dust,
I said ashes to ashes and dust to dust,
If my blues don't get you my jazzing must.

SECOND HAND ROSE

Words by GRANT CLARKE
Music by JAMES F. HANLEY

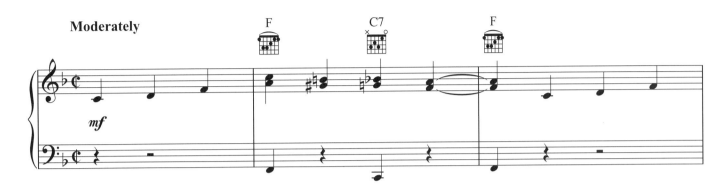

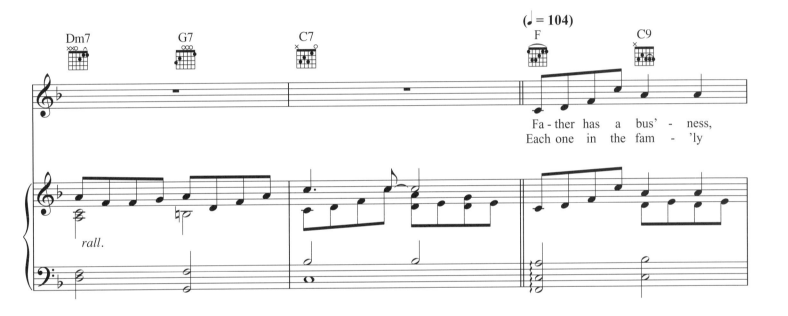

Fa - ther has a bus' - ness,
Each one in the fam - 'ly

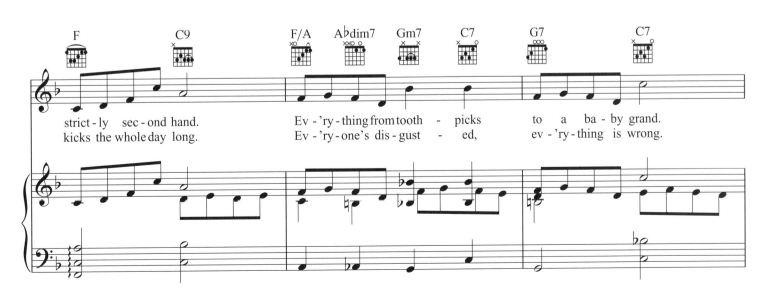

strict - ly sec - ond hand.
kicks the whole day long.
Ev - 'ry - thing from tooth - picks
Ev - 'ry - one's dis - gust - ed,
to a ba - by grand.
ev - 'ry - thing is wrong.

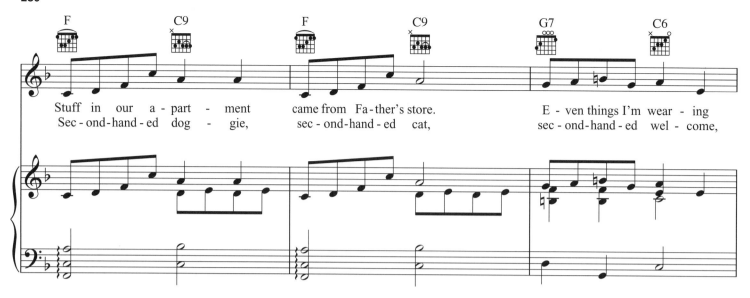

Tempo I

SAY IT WITH MUSIC

Words and Music by
IRVING BERLIN

SENTIMENTAL ME

Words by LORENZ HART
Music by RICHARD RODGERS

SIDE BY SIDE

Words and Music by
HARRY WOODS

295

SLEEPY TIME GAL

Words by JOSEPH ALDEN
and RAYMOND EGAN
Music by ANGELO LORENZO
and RICHARD WHITING

Would-n't it be ___ a change for you and me ___ to stay at home ___ once in a while?
Would-n't it be ___ a pleas-ant sight to see ___ a kitch-en-ette ___ on-ly for you? ___

___ We cab-a-ret ___ un-til the break of day, ___ I'll bet we've
___ Would-n't it be ___ a pleas-ant sight to see ___ a ta-ble

SOFTLY AS IN A MORNING SUNRISE

from THE NEW MOON

Lyrics by OSCAR HAMMERSTEIN II
Music by SIGMUND ROMBERG

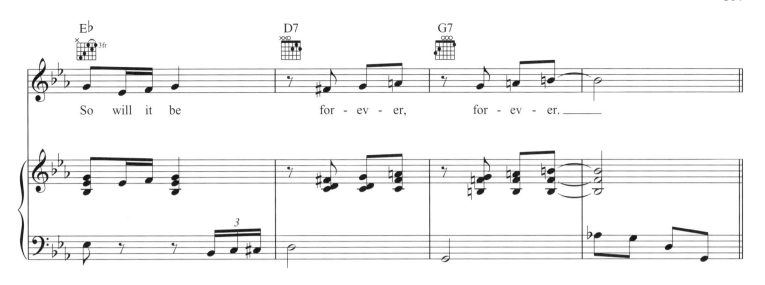

So will it be for - ev - er, for - ev - er. ____

Soft - ly, as in a morn - ing sun - rise, the light of love comes

steal - ing in - to a new - born day, oh!

SOME OF THESE DAYS

Words and Music by
SHELTON BROOKS

SOMEBODY LOVES ME

Music by GEORGE GERSHWIN
Lyrics by B.G. DeSYLVA and BALLARD MacDONALD
French Version by EMELIA RENAUD

SOMEONE TO WATCH OVER ME

from OH, KAY!

Music and Lyrics by GEORGE GERSHWIN
and IRA GERSHWIN

SQUEEZE ME

Words and Music by CLARENCE WILLIAMS
and THOMAS "FATS" WALLER

THE SONG IS ENDED
(But the Melody Lingers On)

Words and Music by
IRVING BERLIN

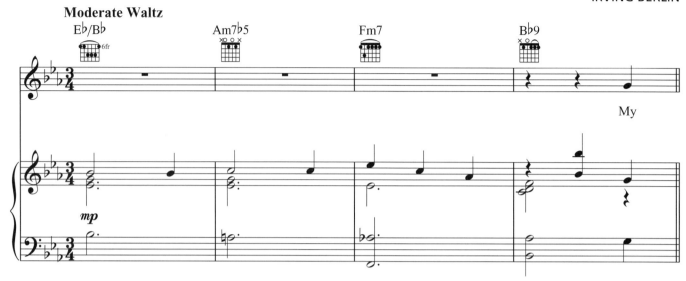

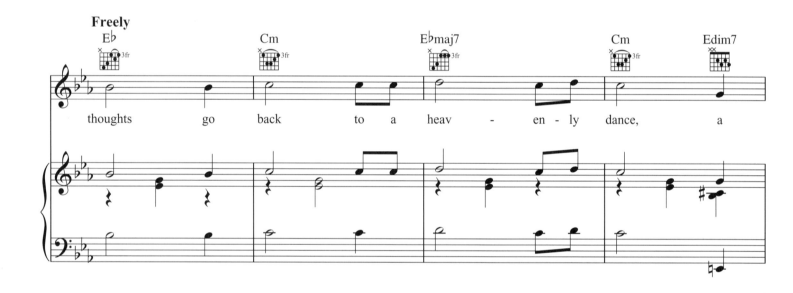

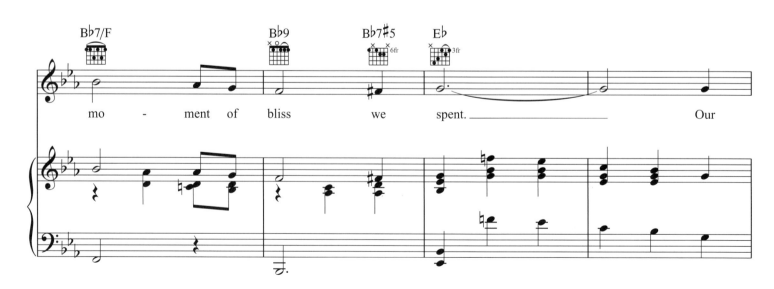

STARDUST

Words by MITCHELL PARISH
Music by HOAGY CARMICHAEL

SWANEE

Words by IRVING CAESAR
Music by GEORGE GERSHWIN

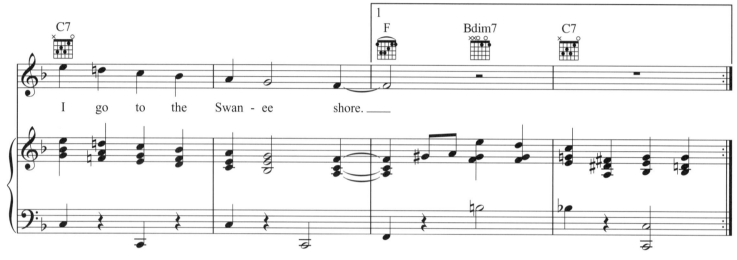

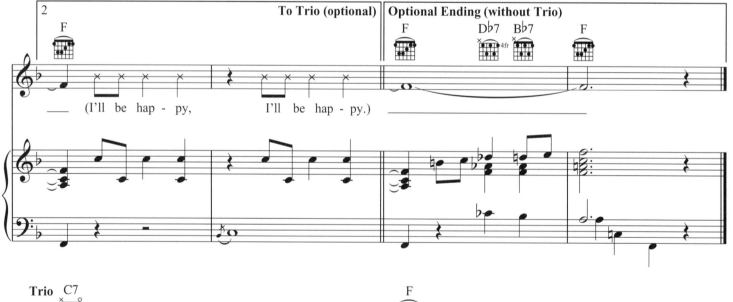

SWEET GEORGIA BROWN

Words and Music by BEN BERNIE,
MACEO PINKARD and KENNETH CASEY

SWEET LORRAINE

Words by MITCHELL PARISH
Music by CLIFF BURWELL

TEA FOR TWO

Words by IRVING CAESAR
Music by VINCENT YOUMANS

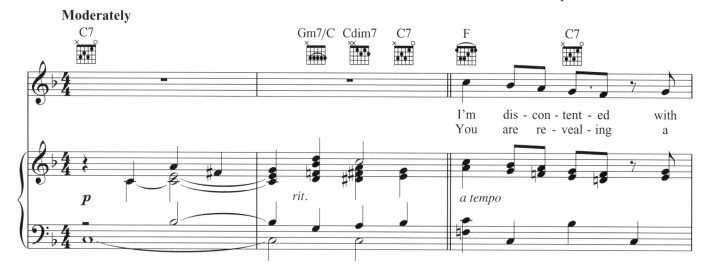

I'm dis-con-tent-ed with
You are re-veal-ing with a

homes that are rent-ed, so I have in-vent-ed my own.
plan so ap-peal-ing, I can't help but feel-ing for you.

Dar-ling, this place is a lov-er's o-a-sis, where life's wea-ry chase is un-
Dar-ling, I planned it. Can't you un-der-stand, it is yours to com-mand it, so

THOU SWELL

from A CONNECTICUT YANKEE
from WORDS AND MUSIC

Words by LORENZ HART
Music by RICHARD RODGERS

THREE O'CLOCK IN THE MORNING

Words by DOROTHY TERRISS
Music by JULIAN ROBLEDO

TIP-TOE THRU' THE TULIPS WITH ME

Words by AL DUBIN
Music by JOE BURKE

356

TOOT, TOOT, TOOTSIE!
(Good-Bye!)

Words and Music by GUS KAHN,
ERNIE ERDMAN, DAN RUSSO
and TED FIORITO

WHISPERING

Words and Music by RICHARD COBURN,
JOHN SCHONBERGER and VINCENT ROSE

'WAY DOWN YONDER IN NEW ORLEANS

Words and Music by HENRY CREAMER
and J. TURNER LAYTON

WHAT'LL I DO?

Words and Music by
IRVING BERLIN

WHEN MY BABY SMILES AT ME

Words and Music by HARRY VON TILZER,
ANDREW B. STERLING, BILL MUNRO
and TED LEWIS

WHEN YOU'RE SMILING
(The Whole World Smiles with You)

Words and Music by MARK FISHER,
JOE GOODWIN and LARRY SHAY

WHO?

from SUNNY

Lyrics by OTTO HARBACH
and OSCAR HAMMERSTEIN II
Music by JEROME KERN

Tom: When a girl's in love with some-one, he must be in-deed a dumb one
Tom: Can't say that I'm sure that I know what you're driv-ing at. *Sunny:* De-ny no

if her se-cret he can-not un-mask.
fur-ther if you choose to feel that way.

Sunny: Then if I'm in love with some-one I must wait un-til there'll come one
Marcia: Make your mind up, don't be shy, no game of ee-nie, mee-nie-mi-no

WHO'S SORRY NOW

Words by BERT KALMAR
and HARRY RUBY
Music by TED SNYDER

You smiled when we part-ed; it hurt me some-how. I thought there was noth-ing worth-while.

The ta-bles are turn-ing and you're cry-ing now, while

I am just learn - ing to smile. _____

Who's sor - ry now? Who's sor - ry now? Whose heart is

ach - ing for break - ing each vow? Who's sad and blue?

Who's cry - ing, too? Just like I cried o - ver you. _____

WITH A SONG IN MY HEART

from SPRING IS HERE

Words by LORENZ HART
Music by RICHARD RODGERS

YES SIR, THAT'S MY BABY

Lyrics by GUS KAHN
Music by WALTER DONALDSON

Who's that com - ing down the street? Who's that look - ing so pe - tite?
Who's the "who" I rave a - bout? Who do I feel blue with - out,

Who's that com - ing down to meet me here? _____
in the win - ter, sum - mer, spring and fall? _____

YES! WE HAVE NO BANANAS

By FRANK SILVER
and IRVING CONN

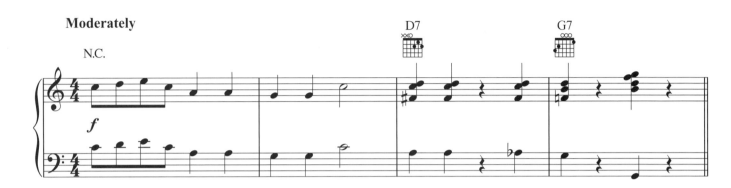

Yes! We have no ba - nan - as. We have no ba-

nan - as to - day. We've string beans and hon - ions, cab-

YOU'RE THE CREAM IN MY COFFEE

Words and Music by B.G. DeSYLVA,
LEW BROWN and RAY HENDERSON

THE ULTIMATE SONGBOOKS

Piano Play-Along

These great songbooks come with our standard arrangements for piano and voice with guitar chord frames plus audio.

The CD includes a full performance of each song, as well as a second track without the piano part so you can play "lead" with the band!

Volumes 86 and beyond also include the Amazing Slow Downer technology so PC and Mac users can adjust the recording to any tempo without changing the pitch!

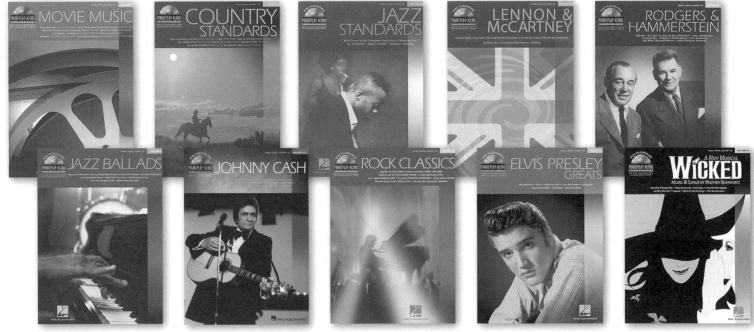

1. MOVIE MUSIC
00311072 P/V/G $14.95

2. JAZZ BALLADS
00311073 P/V/G $14.95

4. BROADWAY CLASSICS
00311075 P/V/G $14.95

5. DISNEY
00311076 P/V/G $14.95

6. COUNTRY STANDARDS
00311077 P/V/G $14.99

7. LOVE SONGS
00311078 P/V/G $14.95

9. CHILDREN'S SONGS
0311080 P/V/G $14.95

10. WEDDING CLASSICS
00311081 Piano Solo $14.95

11. WEDDING FAVORITES
00311097 P/V/G $14.95

12. CHRISTMAS FAVORITES
00311137 P/V/G $15.95

13. YULETIDE FAVORITES
00311138 P/V/G $14.95

14. POP BALLADS
00311145 P/V/G $14.95

15. FAVORITE STANDARDS
00311146 P/V/G $14.95

17. MOVIE FAVORITES
00311148 P/V/G $14.95

18. JAZZ STANDARDS
00311149 P/V/G $14.95

19. CONTEMPORARY HITS
00311162 P/V/G $14.95

20. R&B BALLADS
00311163 P/V/G $14.95

21. BIG BAND
00311164 P/V/G $14.95

22. ROCK CLASSICS
00311165 P/V/G $14.95

23. WORSHIP CLASSICS
00311166 P/V/G $14.95

24. LES MISÉRABLES
00311169 P/V/G $14.95

25. THE SOUND OF MUSIC
00311175 P/V/G $15.99

26. ANDREW LLOYD WEBBER FAVORITES
00311178 P/V/G $14.95

28. LENNON & McCARTNEY
00311180 P/V/G $14.95

29. THE BEACH BOYS
00311181 P/V/G $14.95

30. ELTON JOHN
00311182 P/V/G $14.95

31. CARPENTERS
00311183 P/V/G $14.95

32. BACHARACH & DAVID
00311218 P/V/G $14.95

33. PEANUTS™
00311227 P/V/G $14.95

34. CHARLIE BROWN CHRISTMAS
00311228 P/V/G $15.95

35. ELVIS PRESLEY HITS
00311230 P/V/G $14.95

36. ELVIS PRESLEY GREATS
00311231 P/V/G $14.95

**44. FRANK SINATRA –
POPULAR HITS**
00311277 P/V/G $14.95

**45. FRANK SINATRA –
MOST REQUESTED SONGS**
00311278 P/V/G $14.95

46. WICKED
00311317 P/V/G $16.99

47. RENT
00311319 P/V/G $14.95

48. CHRISTMAS CAROLS
00311332 P/V/G $14.95

49. HOLIDAY HITS
00311333 P/V/G $15.99

50. DISNEY CLASSICS
00311417 P/V/G $14.95

53. GREASE
00311450 P/V/G $14.95

56. THE 1950S
00311459 P/V/G $14.95

61. BILLY JOEL FAVORITES
00311464 P/V/G $14.95

62. BILLY JOEL HITS
00311465 P/V/G $14.95

63. MAROON 5
00316826 P/V/G $14.99

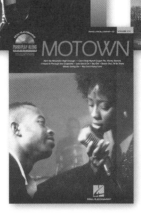

64. GOD BLESS AMERICA
00311489 P/V/G $14.95

65. CASTING CROWNS
00311494 P/V/G $14.95

68. LENNON & McCARTNEY FAVORITES
00311804 P/V/G $14.99

69. PIRATES OF THE CARIBBEAN
00311807 P/V/G $15.99

71. GEORGE GERSHWIN
00102687 P/V/G $24.99

72. VAN MORRISON
00103053 P/V/G $14.99

73. MAMMA MIA! – THE MOVIE
00311831 P/V/G $15.99

74. COLE PORTER
00311844 P/V/G $14.99

75. TWILIGHT
00311860 P/V/G $16.99

76. PRIDE & PREJUDICE
00311862 P/V/G $14.99

77. ELTON JOHN FAVORITES
00311884 P/V/G $14.99

78. ERIC CLAPTON
00311885 P/V/G $14.99

79. TANGOS
00311886 P/V/G $14.99

80. FIDDLER ON THE ROOF
00311887 P/V/G $14.99

81. JOSH GROBAN
00311901 P/V/G $14.99

82. LIONEL RICHIE
00311902 P/V/G $14.99

83. PHANTOM OF THE OPERA
00311903 P/V/G $15.99

84. ANTONIO CARLOS JOBIM FAVORITES
00311919 P/V/G $14.99

85. LATIN FAVORITES
00311920 P/V/G $14.99

86. BARRY MANILOW
00311935 P/V/G $14.99

87. PATSY CLINE
00311936 P/V/G $14.99

88. NEIL DIAMOND
00311937 P/V/G $14.99

89. FAVORITE HYMNS
00311940 P/V/G $14.99

90. IRISH FAVORITES
00311969 P/V/G $14.99

92. DISNEY FAVORITES
00311973 P/V/G $14.99

93. THE TWILIGHT SAGA:
NEW MOON – SOUNDTRACK
00311974 P/V/G $16.99

94. THE TWILIGHT SAGA:
NEW MOON – SCORE
00311975 P/V/G $16.99

95. TAYLOR SWIFT
00311984 P/V/G $14.99

96. BEST OF LENNON & McCARTNEY
00311996 P/V/G $14.99

97. GREAT CLASSICAL THEMES
00312020 PIANO SOLO $14.99

98. CHRISTMAS CHEER
00312021 P/V/G $14.99

99. ANTONIO CARLOS JOBIM CLASSICS
00312039 P/V/G $14.99

100. COUNTRY CLASSICS
00312041 P/V/G $14.99

102. GLEE
00312043 P/V/G $15.99

103. GOSPEL FAVORITES
00312044 P/V/G $14.99

105. BEE GEES
00312055 P/V/G $14.99

106. CAROLE KING
00312056 P/V/G $14.99

107. BOB DYLAN
00312057 P/V/G $16.99

108. SIMON & GARFUNKEL
00312058 P/V/G $16.99

109. TOP HITS
00312068 P/V/G $14.99

110. JUSTIN BIEBER
00109367 P/V/G $14.99

111. STEVIE WONDER
00312119 P/V/G $14.99

112. JOHNNY CASH
00312156 P/V/G $14.99

113. QUEEN
00312164 P/V/G $14.99

114. MOTOWN
00312176 P/V/G $14.99

115. JOHN DENVER
00312249 P/V/G $14.99

116. JAMIE CULLUM
00312275 P/V/G $14.99

117. ALICIA KEYS
00312306 P/V/G $14.99

118. ADELE
00312307 P/V/G $14.99

119. LADY GAGA
00312308 P/V/G $14.99

120. FANTASIA 2000
00312536 PIANO SOLO $14.99

121. NORAH JONES
00306559 P/V/G $19.99

122. WORSHIP HITS
00312564 P/V/G $14.99

123. CHRIS TOMLIN
00312563 P/V/G $14.99

124. WINTER WONDERLAND
00101872 P/V/G $14.99

125. KATY PERRY
00109373 P/V/G $14.99

126. BRUNO MARS
00123121 P/V/G $14.99

127. STAR WARS
00110282 PIANO SOLO $14.99

128. FROZEN
00126480 P/V/G $14.99

HAL•LEONARD®
CORPORATION
7777 W. BLUEMOUND RD. P.O. BOX 13819
MILWAUKEE, WISCONSIN 53213

Visit Hal Leonard Online at
www.halleonard.com

Prices, contents and availability
subject to change without notice.

PEANUTS © United Feature Syndicate, Inc.
Disney characters and artwork © Disney Enterprises, Inc.

1214

THE NEW DECADE SERIES

Books with Online Audio • Arranged for Piano, Voice, and Guitar

The New Decade Series features collections of iconic songs from each decade with great backing tracks so you can play them and sound like a pro. You access the tracks online for streaming or download. **See complete song listings online at www.halleonard.com**

SONGS OF THE 1920s
Ain't Misbehavin' • Baby Face • California, Here I Come • Fascinating Rhythm • I Wanna Be Loved by You • It Had to Be You • Mack the Knife • Ol' Man River • Puttin' on the Ritz • Rhapsody in Blue • Someone to Watch over Me • Tea for Two • Who's Sorry Now • and more.
00137576 P/V/G........................$24.99

SONGS OF THE 1930s
As Time Goes By • Blue Moon • Cheek to Cheek • Embraceable You • A Fine Romance • Georgia on My Mind • I Only Have Eyes for You • The Lady Is a Tramp • On the Sunny Side of the Street • Over the Rainbow • Pennies from Heaven • Stormy Weather (Keeps Rainin' All the Time) • The Way You Look Tonight • and more.
00137579 P/V/G........................$24.99

SONGS OF THE 1940s
At Last • Boogie Woogie Bugle Boy • Don't Get Around Much Anymore • God Bless' the Child • How High the Moon • It Could Happen to You • La Vie En Rose (Take Me to Your Heart Again) • Route 66 • Sentimental Journey • The Trolley Song • You'd Be So Nice to Come Home To • Zip-A-Dee-Doo-Dah • and more.
00137582 P/V/G........................$24.99

SONGS OF THE 1950s
Ain't That a Shame • Be-Bop-A-Lula • Chantilly Lace • Earth Angel • Fever • Great Balls of Fire • Love Me Tender • Mona Lisa • Peggy Sue • Que Sera, Sera (Whatever Will Be, Will Be) • Rock Around the Clock • Sixteen Tons • A Teenager in Love • That'll Be the Day • Unchained Melody • Volare • You Send Me • Your Cheatin' Heart • and more.
00137595 P/V/G........................$24.99

SONGS OF THE 1960s
All You Need Is Love • Beyond the Sea • Born to Be Wild • California Girls • Dancing in the Street • Happy Together • King of the Road • Leaving on a Jet Plane • Louie, Louie • My Generation • Oh, Pretty Woman • Sunshine of Your Love • Under the Boardwalk • You Really Got Me • and more.
00137596 P/V/G......................$24.99

SONGS OF THE 1970s
ABC • Bridge over Troubled Water • Cat's in the Cradle • Dancing Queen • Free Bird • Goodbye Yellow Brick Road • Hotel California • I Will Survive • Joy to the World • Killing Me Softly with His Song • Layla • Let It Be • Piano Man • The Rainbow Connection • Stairway to Heaven • The Way We Were • Your Song • and more.
00137599 P/V/G $27.99

SONGS OF THE 1980s
Africa • Beat It • Careless Whisper • Come on Eileen • Don't Stop Believin' • Every Rose Has Its Thorn • Footloose • I Just Called to Say I Love You • Jessie's Girl • Livin' on a Prayer • Saving All My Love for You • Take on Me • Up Where We Belong • The Wind Beneath My Wings • and more.
00137600 P/V/G........................$27.99

SONGS OF THE 1990s
Angel • Black Velvet • Can You Feel the Love Tonight • (Everything I Do) I Do It for You • Friends in Low Places • Hero • I Will Always Love You • More Than Words • My Heart Will Go On (Love Theme from 'Titanic') • Smells like Teen Spirit • Under the Bridge • Vision of Love • Wonderwall • and more.
00137601 P/V/G........................$27.99

SONGS OF THE 2000s
Bad Day • Beautiful • Before He Cheats • Chasing Cars • Chasing Pavements • Drops of Jupiter (Tell Me) • Fireflies • Hey There Delilah • How to Save a Life • I Gotta Feeling • I'm Yours • Just Dance • Love Story • 100 Years • Rehab • Unwritten • You Raise Me Up • and more.
00137608 P/V/G........................$27.99

HAL•LEONARD® CORPORATION

7777 W. BLUEMOUND RD. P.O. BOX 13819 MILWAUKEE, WI 53213

halleonard.com

Prices, content, and availability subject to change without notice.